```
J 940.531 Ste
Steele, D. Kelley
Would you salute?
```

```
            CY      JAN 07
                      $22.95
1st ed.         ocm57541791
```

HARRIS COUNTY PUBLIC LIBRARY
CROSBY BRANCH LIBRARY

A MESSAGE FROM THE AUTHOR

This is the story of Margot and her family's experiences in Germany during the Holocaust. I met Margot several years ago and was immediately drawn to her smile and sweet face. Her story touched me.

I have always studied the Holocaust with bewilderment, not understanding how everyday people stood by and watched as their neighbors and friends were robbed, beaten, and destroyed. Surely you and I would have reacted differently. . . . Wouldn't we?

When Margot shared her story with me, it was different than any I had heard. The struggle for love, self-preservation, and sacrifice that occurred in this one family captivated me. While *Would You Salute?* is the story of just one girl's experiences during the Holocaust, maybe it can help us understand how hatred and fear can grow.

This was a difficult story for me to write. I have tried to be truthful without overwhelming the student reader with so much information they cannot step into the story and think and feel. My hope is, this story will be a tool for teaching empathy and that it will encourage children and adults to think about what they would and would not do. I believe it is this knowledge that will help us be kinder to one another.

To those of you who select this book with the intention of learning and teaching, remember the words of Helen Keller: "I am only one, but I am still one. I cannot do everything but still I can do something. And because I cannot do everything I will not refuse to do the something that I can do."

D. Kelley Steele

Would You Salute?

by D. Kelley Steele
illustrated by Becky Hyatt Rickenbaker

HIDDEN PATH PUBLICATIONS
STATESVILLE, NORTH CAROLINA

Text Copyright © 2005 D. Kelley Steele
Illustrations Copyright © 2005 Becky Hyatt Rickenbaker

All rights reserved.

FIRST EDITION

Published by Hidden Path Publications, Inc.
    304 Brierwood Rd.
    Statesville, NC 28677
    704-878-6986
    www.hiddenpathpub.com
    dkelleysteele@aol.com

Produced by Barbara Stone
    WRITTEN IN STONE
    832 Pasture Lane
    Orangeburg, SC 29118
    803-533-5688
    pasturelane@bellsouth.net

Printed in Korea

Publisher's Cataloging-in-Publication
(Provided by Quality Books, Inc.)

Steele, D. Kelley.
    Would you salute? / by D. Kelley Steele.
    p. cm.
    SUMMARY: The true story of a young girl who grew up in Germany. Her life was like any child's—until Hitler.
    ISBN 0-9711534-2-6

    1. Children of interfaith marriage—Germany—Biography—Juvenile literature. 2. Holocaust, Jewish (1939-1945)—Germany—Personal narratives—Juvenile literature. 3. Germany—Biography—Juvenile literature.
[1. Children of interfaith marriage—Germany—Biography.
2. Holocaust, Jewish (1939-1945) 3. Germany—Biography.]
I. Title.

DS135.G5S74 2005   940.53'18'092
                           QBI05-800164

For Margot and for her Mother and Father
We will remember your strength,
love, and devotion for one another
each time we read your story.
D.K.S.

For Margot Wimpfheimer and Don Pike
Both survivors of WWII

B.H.R.

If you could hear my voice, you would know that I am an old woman. My words shake a little when I talk, and my once-thick accent has been softened by the years. Sometimes when I peer into the mirror, I am surprised by the white hair and the deep wrinkles in the face staring back at me. You see, in my heart, I am still a young girl running and playing through the streets as my father chases me. I have many memories of my childhood in Germany—some good, some not so good.

It is hard to know when the good times stopped and the not-so-good times began. It is like that sometimes, even now. My memories come and go.

I remember hearing *his* name for the first time.... Hitler. I was sitting in class when Teacher spoke of him—Adolf Hitler.

I was just like you. Hitler was a name—only a name. It meant nothing to me. Just a man somewhere, not here. But, that name was about to change my whole life.

Teacher taught us a new salute we would do every day. The salute was to show respect for this man called Hitler and to show that we supported his ideas for our country.

So, we saluted. . . . I saluted.

Every morning in class, we saluted.

Would you have saluted?

While new things were happening at school, home was still the same. My father was a doctor. His office was on the first floor of our house. I remember him as being a good, kind man. He almost never took money from his patients. He would help them with whatever ailed them, sometimes give *them* money, and send them on their way. Most of his patients were poor, but my father did not care. He was a doctor because he wanted to help.

My father loved to play with me. He taught me to ski and to swim. On Saturdays, I would hold his hand and walk with him to the synagogue to worship and thank God for our blessings.

My mother worked hard in our home. She loved me and my daddy very much and took care of us. On Sundays, I would hold her hand and walk with her to the church to worship and thank God for our blessings.

At school, things kept changing. Sometimes, Teacher would take us out into the streets and tell us to salute as the soldiers marched by. I saluted. We all saluted. Would you have saluted?

Students started wearing uniforms. Most of my friends wore them. I did not want to be different. And the uniforms looked smart. I put one on. At the end of the day, I marched home, so proud of the way I looked in my new uniform. Would you feel proud?

I marched straight up the steps of our home to show my mother and father. Opening the door, I stared straight into the eyes of my mother. I was smiling so big! . . . But, she was not smiling back.

I still remember her words to me, "Take those off now! You have no idea what you are doing."

Her harsh voice puzzled me. She sounded angry and sad like I had done something wrong. But I did not know what I had done.

"Mother, all of my friends, everyone is wearing this. Why can't I?" I asked.

That day I heard my mother speak the name Hitler for the first time.

The more she talked, the dirtier the uniform made me feel. Hitler was a man who not only wanted to control Germany, but he also wanted to control how Germans thought. Hitler did not like Jews, and he wanted all Germans to hate Jews.
    I never wanted to wear the uniform again.

Soon my family's life changed. My father was no longer allowed to take care of his patients. But sometimes, at night, he would sneak out and visit them in their homes. It was not long before guards stood outside our door with their guns so that father could not be a doctor.

My mother was not Jewish. Her brother came to her one day and announced that he must join Hitler's army and become a Nazi. My uncle cried when he told her, because he loved my father. Uncle did not want to join, but he was afraid his family would be hurt if he did not. My mother turned away from him and said, "Do not come back here."

Things got worse for my family and for many other families. People I had known all my life suddenly started calling me names. "You filthy Jew!" they shouted. My friends no longer played with me. They were afraid to be seen playing with the daughter of a Jew. They were afraid the soldiers would hurt them.

But, sometimes, they would stand on the street across from my house and wave quickly at me before anyone could see.

Mother and I stopped going to church on Sunday. Many of the Christians would no longer talk to us. Some even said mean things. Mother began going to the synagogue with Father on Saturday to show her support and love for him. They left me at home to make sure I was safe.

Home was not safe for long. Nazi soldiers began coming into our house and stealing our things. They took paintings and furniture. They took jewelry and clothes. They took anything they wanted.

Soon, they began taking my father. I cried as I watched him being driven away. My mother would hold me and say, "Be strong. Pray."

The Nazis would keep my father for hours, sometimes days, and then send him home.

I was very afraid. I was afraid something would happen to my father—and to me, because I was half Jewish. My mother's courage amazed me. When the soldiers came and banged on our door, I would hide behind her, my legs trembling. But she would say to them, "Leave us alone, you Nazi pigs."

One day my mother was sweeping in front of our house. She saw a Jewish man walking down the street. She watched and listened as a soldier yelled cruel things at him. Many people watched. Would you watch?

My mother could no longer do nothing.
　She ran across the street and hit the soldier. Before the soldier could turn on my mother, some of the people watching dragged her into their house and hid her.

Uncle still came to visit us. Because he loved my father, he would not wear the Nazi uniform in our home.
  He would even call to warn us when Nazi soldiers were coming to steal our things and to take Father.

I believe the soldiers let my father go so many times because my uncle told them to.

One day Uncle came to us and told my father the soldiers were coming again, but this time they were also taking Mother and me.

My dear father loved us so much. He did not want anything bad to happen to us. That same day, he left our home, taking some special medicine along with him. He swallowed the medicine and went to sleep. He never awoke again.

When the people in our town found out about my father, they came to our home. Many of them wept. Even some of the soldiers cried because my father had taken care of them when they were sick.

After my father died, the Nazi guards no longer stood outside our door. My father had saved us. He was such a good man.

The soldiers still marched through our streets. People still saluted—but I could no longer raise my arm. I could no longer salute, because I understood what the salute meant.

Would YOU salute?

Margot was born October 8, 1920, in the town of Karlshrue, Germany. She was an only child and dreamed of having brothers and sisters. Her father, Otto, was a medical doctor and had his office on the first level of their home. Her mother, Hildegard, took care of the house and supported her husband in his practice.

Margot loved all sports and was very athletic. Her father taught her to ski and swim. Her favorite activity, though, was gathering her friends from school and the neighborhood and taking them to her house for cookies and hot chocolate.

Margot's father died in 1937. In 1939, Margot and her mother came to the United States to live and settled in New York. Margot quickly learned English and began giving speeches about the destruction that Hitler and his Nazi army were creating. Margot's mother worked very hard, taking all the jobs she could find to support the two of them. She mostly cleaned houses. Margot says she could not have survived all she faced had it not been for her mother.

Margot gave birth to her first child in 1940. She had always promised her mother she would give her lots of grandchildren. She kept her promise and went on to have nine more children. Margot's mother, Hildegard, lived to be just two weeks shy of her one-hundredth birthday.

Today, Margot lives in North Carolina. She has thirty-four grandchildren and twenty-four great-grandchildren. In her bedroom, beside her bed, stands a picture of her mother and father—the same picture you see in this book.

Margot with her mother in 1984. Her mother was 99 years old.

Margot and her daughter

Margot visited Germany in the 1980s and photographed her home. The three-story home extends the length of three windows on either side of the doorway.

Margot and family ~ 2001

Margot's Memories

This picture of Margot's father, Otto, and mother, Hildegard, rests on her bedside table.

Margot at 8 or 9 months

Margot at 8 or 9 years.

Margot and her parents at a cafe in Germany

Margot and friends at the swimming pool

Margot and her firstborn child, 1940

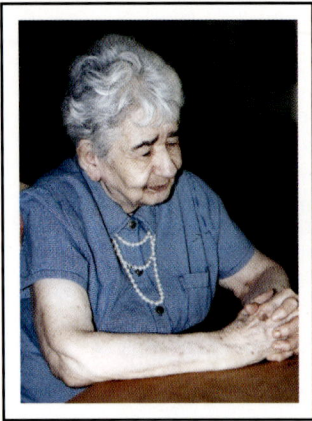   

Margot says she is happy this story about her family was written. "Working with the author helped bring back all the memories of that time—especially the good ones."

When Margot was asked why this story is so important to tell, she said, "So the people will know what is right in here [*pointing to her heart*] and not go along so easily with what others are doing."

photos by Becky Hyatt Rickenbaker

Harris County Public Library
Houston, Texas